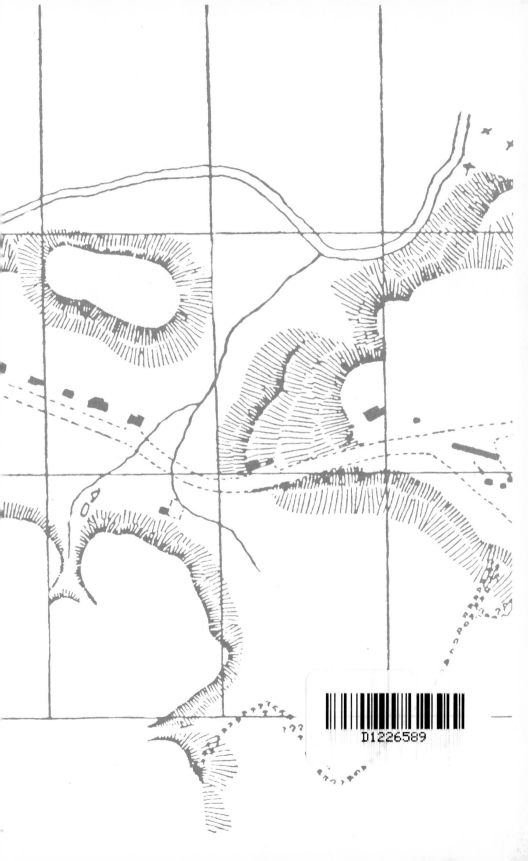

First Winter

Washington and His Army in Morristown, 1777

JAMES ELLIOTT LINDSLEY

THE TRUSTEES OF THE MORRISTOWN GREEN INC.
MORRISTOWN, NEW JERSEY
2006

The Trustees of the Morristown Green acknowledge the generous grant

for funding the design of this publication from the

MORRISTOWN AND MORRIS TOWNSHIP LIBRARY

ISBN-13: 978-0-9788613-0-8
ISBN-10: 0-9788613-0-2

PUBLISHED BY
THE TRUSTEES OF THE MORRISTOWN GREEN INC.
MORRISTOWN, NEW JERSEY

Book and jacket design by Robert Shubert of Triart Graphics, Inc. Cedar Knolls, NJ

Illustrations and graphics by Brian Bilby and David Nilsen of Triart Graphics, Inc. Cedar Knolls, NJ

Printed by The Stinehour Press, Lunenburg, VT

For My Grandson, Baxter:

Historian-in-the-making

Also by James Elliott Lindsley

A Certain Splendid House

27 Elm Street

This Planted Vine

The Silent Procession

Table of Contents

Acknowledgements

$\mathscr{I}$ am grateful to the librarians at SUNY New Paltz, N.Y. and the librarian of the Century Association of New York for their help and courtesy. Eric P. Olsen, Historian at Morristown National Historical Park confirmed my dates of Washington's four known visits to Morristown, and I thank him for his help. I am glad the Green Vision Committee brought the subject of the first winter to my attention, and I appreciate the trust they placed in me to write about it. The Committee arranged with Susan Gulick, the Director of the Morristown and Morris Township Library, for the use of its facilities and I want to acknowledge the helpfulness of Director Gulick and Christine Jochem, the Department Head of the North Jersey History Center at that Library. Once more, Cam Cavanaugh has been of great help. Her keen knowledge of how to use the English language is matched by her accurate information about our history. Together with many others, I owe her deep thanks. Finally, I have to thank my wife, Barbara, for guiding me through the idiosyncrasies of computerland.

James Elliott Lindsley
May, 2006

Preface

The Trustees of the Morristown Green, Inc. and their Green Vision Committee asked me to prepare a study of Washington's first stay in Morristown. Through the years, the second encampment of the Continental Army, 1779-1780, has been given preeminent attention for reasons I have suggested in this little book. This has been especially true since the establishment of the Morristown National Historical Park, which draws the public's attention to sites commemorating the second encampment: the Ford mansion, its adjoining museum, and the campsite at Jockey Hollow.

The first winter, 1777, is marked by no building. Perhaps its "monument" is the Morristown Green, for it was on the Green that the soldiers paraded, and it was in the buildings facing the Green that Continental officers had their headquarters.

This study concentrates on the winter of 1777 when Washington and the remnants of his army were in Morristown. Our scope will be limited to the major events and concerns of Washington's headquarters in the Arnold Tavern at the very center of Morristown: the Green. The aim of this book is to tell the story of Washington and his army – what there was of it! – in the winter months of 1777, and explain why it was a seminal time in our nation's history.

First Winter

In the autumn of 1776 the American army suffered a series of humiliating defeats on Long Island, Manhattan, and Westchester. "I feel mad, vexed, sick and sorry", General Greene wrote to Henry Knox.[1] Barely managing to keep his troops, now reduced to maybe 3,000 men, together, Washington finally managed to lead them out of Westchester, cross the Hudson, and march south. Where would they go now that winter was setting in?

Both Newark and New Brunswick were considered as suitable locations to over-winter, but they were too close to the enemy forces to be safe. With few options, and running out of time to find a location, Washington decided to head to Philadelphia. The army made camp on the Pennsylvania bank of the Delaware River. It was there that Washington made the momentous decision to turn his

army around, cross the Delaware at midnight on Christmas Eve, and launch a surprise attack on the Hessian-held town of Trenton. After taking Trenton, he moved on Princeton and defeated the British army there.

His unexpected victories in the battles at Trenton and Princeton shocked the British and brought hope to the Continental Army. Tired but galvanized, the army moved on to Morristown, where they would spend the winter. What is now the Morristown Green was central to their operations there, and the adjacent Arnold Tavern served as Washington's headquarters over the long winter of 1777.

MORRISTOWN

The Green and Its Surroundings

$\mathcal{I}$t would have taken some imagination to call it the Green in 1777. At that time it was "a vacant and nearly square lot comprised in the large tract of land then owned by the Presbyterian church".[2] It was set apart as a public space soon after Morristown was settled in the early years of the 18th century, but horse and human traffic prevented the growth of much vegetation. "No grass grew on its face", says a Morristown historian.[3]

The map commissioned by Washington soon after his arrival in 1777 (shown on the next page) has several roads running diagonally across the open space. One road led toward Jockey Hollow and beyond, to Mendham. Another road led

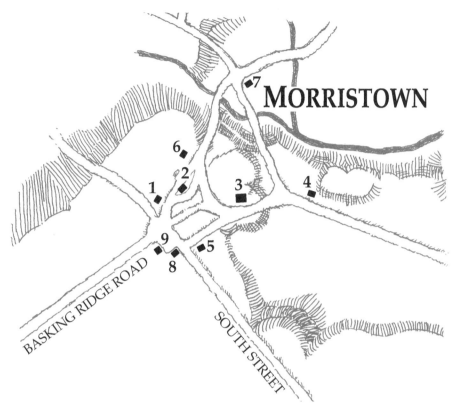

The map commissioned by General Washington and drawn by Colonel Robert Erskine shows places mentioned in the text.

The above identifies the following: 1) the Arnold Tavern; 2) Court House; 3) Presbyterian Church; 4) Presbyterian parsonage; 5) General Greene's quarters; 6) Baptist Church; 7) Dickerson Tavern; 8) Continental Store House; 9) Parade Ground.

down "the gully" (Water Street) to a cluster of buildings in what had been the original settlement of Morristown. Another "road" (it was probably no more than a horse path) skirted behind the county court house.

The first court house – "a rude log structure" – was built

on the Green in 1755.[4] It was replaced by a new court house seven years prior to Washington's arrival in January of 1777. In two meetings of the church trustees held in May and June of 1770 the county Freeholders were given permission to build the new court house near or on the site of the 1755 building. A second floor and bold cupola were added in 1775. The narrow lane on the west side of the Green separating the court house from the building across the way was called Court Street. It retained that name until a new court house was built on Washington Street in 1827.

The Morris County Courthouse on the Green diagonally across the road from Washington's headquarters in the Arnold Tavern. The second floor and cupola were built just prior to the army's first stay in Morristown. The Erskine map shows an ancillary building beside it which may have been a jail.

There was a public well directly behind the court house which was still there in 1905. A pillory at about the center of the present Green was conspicuously located so as to be seen by passers-by. Trees in situ are said to have been used as gibbets, when needed.

The main road leading to Morristown and its Green was then, as now, called Morris Street. Its significant houses are shown on the map Washington commissioned. First, about a mile from the Green, was the house of "Squire" Benjamin Lindsley. His next door neighbor, my progenitor, Joseph Lindsley, was a distant relation. Immediately to the west was the new, imposing house of Jacob Ford, Jr. Moving closer to the Green, at a distance of about half a mile, the map showed the house of Jabez Canfield which was then a one-story house facing the road. Much later, the house was enlarged and moved perhaps fifty feet back from the road to front on present day Olyphant Place. This was where General Schuyler lived, and where Alexander Hamilton successfully courted the Schuyler's daughter, Betsy.

Next, as one approached town, was the house of Frederick King, who served as a quartermaster in the war. Close by, the home of Mahlon Ford, a cousin of Jacob Ford, Jr., was next to the house thought to belong to Peter Dickerson, an early agitator for Colonial independence. Dickerson was a carpenter, a tavern proprietor, and a militia man, and was thus frequently called away to fight in the skirmishes that became a vital factor of patriot aggression in 1777.

Then there was the home of Col. Joseph Lewis and next, at the foot of the hill ascending to the Green, was the parsonage of Lewis's father-in-law, Timothy Johnes, the minister in Morristown's

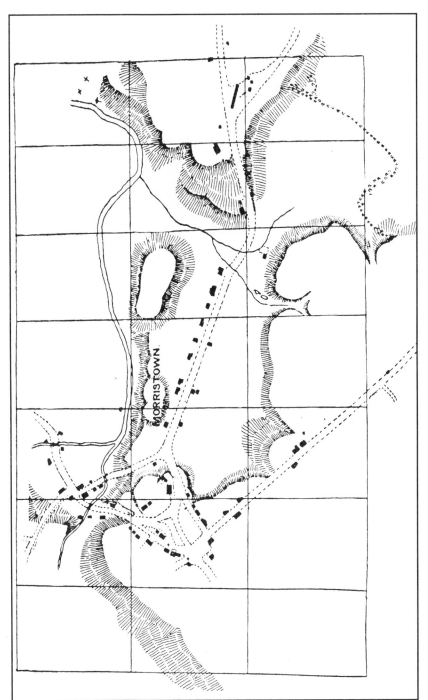

Plan of Morristown by survey ordered by General Washington, 1777.

Presbyterian church since 1742. The church was located on the northeast corner of the Green, across from the Baptist church on the northwest corner. Both churches were used as military hospitals beginning in the winter of 1777 and for the duration of military activity in the area. Each of the houses along the way probably housed as many officers of the army as the families could manage to take in. All the houses had vegetable gardens and barns for fowl and cattle. Farms farther away from the Green produced wheat, corn, rye, oats, vegetables and some fruits.[5]

The Baptist Church, used as a hospital during the war. It stood at the corner of the Green on the brow of the hill descending to the Whippany River. There was no Speedwell Avenue in 1777.

Other buildings faced the Green-one or more stores and the house of Col. Henry Remsen between the Baptist church and the Arnold Tavern on the west side, and the "Continental Stores" on the south. This building, possibly erected immediately after the army reached Morristown as a repository for military material, was conveniently located diagonally across the road from the occasional headquarters of General Nathaniel Greene, Washington's Quartermaster. (He also lived in Basking Ridge, possibly because it was nearer "Vealtown" – present-day Bernardsville – and its food stores.)

Going east from there on the road that led to Bottle Hill (Madison) now called South Street, there were two sizeable dwellings. The one on the right was occupied by Lt. Col. William

The Continental Store House on the Green next to the parade ground. There were probably other storage buildings in the vicinity but this major one survived to become O'Hara's Tavern.

DeHart, whose two brothers were killed in the Revolutionary War. DeHart was a lawyer, and he supervised the jail.[6] A bit further, on the north side of the road, was the house of Samuel Tuthill. He was closely related to both Jacob Arnold and Jacob Ford, and after the war he was County Clerk and a judge.

It is easy to see, then, that the people who lived on or near the Green and Washington's headquarters in that winter of 1777 were all, one way or another, preoccupied by the anxieties of the war. A well-equipped enemy was not far away, and American soldiers were conspicuous in the village. The Continental army was, however, diminished by expiring enlistments, and the soldiers that remained were poorly clothed and fed. A shrewd observer might note that the military problem was compounded by a state militia that sometimes resented Continental orders. The patriot triumphs at Trenton and Princeton at the dawn of the new year, however, brought hope and a renewed enthusiasm for the war to the somewhat dispirited populace.

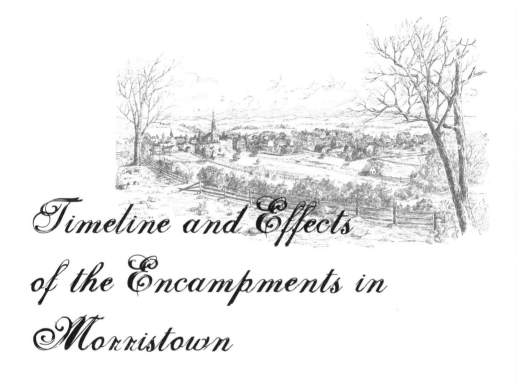

Timeline and Effects of the Encampments in Morristown

Washington's army was in and around Morristown through all the years of the Revolutionary War. The small village of no more than 250 inhabitants "it is said"[7] was in the years 1776 to 1782 subject to an increase of men, horses and cattle that would have been impossible to bear apart from the emergencies of war. Prices soared. Shoes rose from two to twenty-five shillings. Local farmers were known to inflate their prices, and were reluctant to sell anything to the army on credit.[8] It was said they set two prices, one for hard currency and another, 15% higher, for the script authorized by Congress.[9] This is understandable, for Continental money was of unreliable value, whereas the civilians could depend upon the accustomed English Pound or the Spanish dollar.[10]

We know Washington himself appeared in Morristown four times during the war, and that he had been in Basking Ridge as Lord Stirling's guest earlier, in 1773.[11] The first time Washington came with the troops was during this first 1777 encampment when, somewhat unwillingly, he set up headquarters in Morristown. To his own surprise, he remained almost five months, and returned for a brief stay early in July. The third visit, the famous second encampment, was when the army was quartered in Morristown from December, 1779 to late June the following year. In that arduous winter Washington and his "military family" (a group of Washington's officers, aides, and personal guard) occupied the house of Theodosia Ford while most of the army was camped in Jockey Hollow. His fourth appearance was in November, 1781, after General Cornwallis surrendered at Yorktown. Of this fourth time in Morristown, March 28th, 1782, it might quite literally be said, "Washington Slept Here" – for the next day he moved on toward West Point and to what in a short time would be a farewell to his army and his officers. But his visit was not short enough to prevent the Magistrates of Morris County from catching up with him to remind him that their 1780 request for payment for the damages done to the court house by the army had so far not been met.

The Arnold Tavern, Washington's First Headquarters

The encampment of 1779-80 is fairly well known and researched. This is probably because Washington's headquarters, the house Jacob Ford, Jr. built, was, fortuitously purchased and preserved as a museum in 1873. The United States was at that time making plans to celebrate its Centennial and US history; hitherto the province of only a few, turned into a national interest.

It is easy to trace the subsequent local emphasis that was

placed on that winter of 1779-80. First, there was the drama and sufferings of the ill-clothed, ill-fed soldiers in that terrible winter. It was said to be the worst in the 18th century (although 1777 wasn't much better). Then, there was the handsome Ford house itself – saved from probable destruction in 1873, it was fitted up as a museum exhibiting some furniture that Washington used when he lived in the house and some "Colonial relics" that were either contributed by members and friends of the Washington Association of New Jersey or, on rare occasions, purchased by the Association's trustees who owned and managed the house. At the annual dinner meetings of the Washington Association learned speeches were presented describing the winter encampments of 1777 and 1779-80.

In contrast to the celebrity of the Ford mansion, there was little notice given Washington's headquarters during the first winter encampment – Jacob Arnold's tavern on the Green. Its importance as the site of some of the most seminal moments of Washington's military and administrative leadership was ignored. The Ford house, on the other hand, grew in fame. For years prior to its purchase by the Washington Association, it was something of a mecca for history enthusiasts who knew Washington had lived there.

The Arnold Tavern was slow to receive such respect. A County history in 1882 stated, "This historic building is still standing, though considerably altered."[12] The tavern had a dismal decline in the 19th century. The visiting public demanded more luxury than a casual tavern could offer. For a time, it was famous only for its bear-baiting shows in the back yard.

Following a gradual decline as a hostelry the first floor was divided into three stores in the mid-19th century. A photograph of the building taken just before its removal in 1886 shows a plain, business building. It was painted yellow then, with green Venetian shutters. A sketch of the tavern as it was supposed to

The Arnold Tavern as it was remembered in the late 19th century. The Assembly Room wing is shown accurately, but it is possible the long porch and third floor were added some time after the winter of 1777.

look in Washington's time showed a porch running the length of the building, but if it had ever been there it was gone by 1880.

The owner at the time was a haberdasher named Philip Hoffman. His shop was located on the north side of the building, next to Crowell's jewelry store, which occupied most of the original broad center hall. Adams' and Fairchild's grocery was on the south side.

Philip Hoffman's family had lived in Morris County for generations. He had a genuine respect for local history, a quality he passed on to his son, Henry, who succeeded him in the haberdashery and, after retirement, wrote a weekly column of local history for the newspaper. But Hoffman was doing business in a town whose commercial growth after the Civil War was inexorably sweeping away old buildings that appeared to have outlived their usefulness. That is why there remain no very old buildings on or near Morristown Green today. Even the two 18th-century churches were removed, one for commercial reasons, and the other because its Classic presence was out of style in 1893.

In the mid-1880s Phillip Hoffman said he planned to demolish the Arnold Tavern and put up another building on its site. Fortunately for what had once been Washington's headquarters, however, he came upon a way to save the historic old building by finding as its buyer an enterprising woman, Julia Keese Colles. She was a Morristown hostess and lecturer, married to a man who inherited property that once belonged to General John Doughty.

When Colles purchased the Arnold Tavern building from Hoffman, she intended to move it onto another site and convert it into a hostelry named "Colonial House". It is so named on an 1887 map of Morristown. The move was made, with considerable difficulty, as the local newspapers noted. The vacated space on the Green enabled Phillip Hoffman to put up his new brick business building on the site of the tavern in 1886. He named it "The Arnold", and had those words inscribed in a granite lintel.

The old tavern, though it was elaborately renovated after the Colonial Revival fashion of the time, never became a hotel. After it was relocated on the Colles estate, on the east side of Mt. Kemble Avenue next to what was then named Schuyler (now Colles) Avenue about a mile from its original site, the now-grand "hotel" stood vacant for several years. Then it was purchased to become the first All Souls' Hospital. It was destroyed by fire in April, 1918.

Colles recorded events up to the tavern's purchase by the Hospital Association in her unique 1893 book, *Authors and Writers Associated with Morristown*. Hers is the best description we have of the tavern as it stood before its destruction:

> *The [Arnold Tavern] with its many associations was about to be destroyed, when it was rescued, at the suggestion of the author of this book, and restored upon its present site on the Colles estate, on Mt. Kemble avenue, the old Baskingridge road of the Revolution. It has recently [1893] been purchased and occupied for a hospital by the All Souls' Hospital Association. Though*

1777

extended and enlarged, it is still the same building and retains many of the distinctive features which characterized it when the residence of Washington. Here is still the bedroom which Washington occupied, the parlor, the dining-room and the ball-room where he received his generals, Greene, Knox, Schuyler, Gates, Lee, deKalb, Steuben, Wayne, Winds, Putnam, Sullivan and others, besides distinguished visitors from abroad, all of whom met here continually during the winter of 1777 ... In one of the bedrooms of this old house has been seen, within a few years, between the floor and the ceiling below, a long case for guns, above

Nathanael Greene

Henry Knox

Philip Schuyler

Horatio Gates

Charles Lee

which was painted on the floor, in very large squares, covering the entire opening, a checker-board about which, in an emergency, evidently the soldiers expected to sit and so conceal from the enemy the trap door of their arsenal...[13]

The significance of the Arnold Tavern would have been well noted had the fortunes of the place been different. For instance, if the tavern had become a museum or if it had been maintained as a top-quality inn, its occupancy by Washington in his first winter in Morristown would have been made known.

Johann De Kalb

*Friedrich Wilhelm
Van Stuben*

Anthony Wayne

Israel Putnam

John Sullivan

What the Early Historians Said

ow we will examine what local historians wrote in the 19th century. The first of our historians is Rufus S. Green. Green was influenced by Joseph F. Tuttle, who had written in the 1850s, and in addition, he tells us he had other "materials placed in his hand".[14] Both Green and Tuttle were Presbyterian clergymen and, we assume, had congregants who remembered, or whose parents remembered, the War of Independence. Green's chapter titled "Morristown" appeared in the broadly circulated Munsell's *Morris County*, published in 1882.

Green emphasizes the presence of iron mines and works near Morristown. He states that Washington told Richard Henry

Lee "in Morris County there are between 80 and 100 iron works, large and small".[15] A modern historian states that there were three large mines and twelve small ones in Morris County. They produced the metal that 44 area forges wrought into kettles, pots, cooking utensils, plows, rakes, wheels and other ironware.[16] These ironworks included the one owned by Jacob Arnold at Speedwell.

Rufus Green emphatically states, "Arnold kept the hotel in Morristown where, in January, 1777, Washington took up his winter quarters, and which is still [1882] standing, on the

Ironworks circa 1777 and a selection of items that would have been forged.

northwest side of the public square".[17] He also asserts, without attribution, that the existence of a powder mill in Morristown was the "main reason" Washington set up headquarters in Morristown in 1777.[18] It is also Rufus Green who states Washington participated in the Communion in the "dell" behind the Presbyterian parsonage on Morris Street (the Presbyterian church being at the time occupied by convalescing soldiers),[19] and he says "tradition relates" Washington, in what was thought

The Presbyterian Church as conceived by a 19th century artist. It has never been determined whether the steeple was at the end of the building or midpoint astride its roof. The church was used as a hospital and possibly for other military-related purposes throughout the war.

to be serious illness, appointed General Nathaniel Greene to succeed him.[20] Here also is the account of Alexander Hamilton deceiving the Tory spy in General Greene's office. He credits a local man with that story, General Doughty, who told it to his neighbor, George P. Macculloch.[21] Rufus Green also locates General Greene's office on the southeast corner of the Green. Research for this study suggests it had been the home of Tory Nicholas Hoffman until he fled to New York.

More to the point, however, is Rufus Green's quoting Washington as writing of Morristown that "the situation is by no means favorable to our views, and as soon as the purposes are answered for which we came I think to remove, though I confess I do not know how we shall procure covering for our men elsewhere".[22]

Julia Keese Colles also includes some generally accepted

General Green's quarters as the building appeared in the 19th century when a full third story was added.

truths about the winter of 1777 in "Historic Morristown", the prefatory chapter to her 1893 book about Morristown writers in 1893. She describes the encampment "in the valley bearing the beautiful Indian name of 'Lowantica' [where the] terrible scourge of small-pox broke out among the soldiers". She describes the death of the Jacob Fords, son and father, Washington's serious illness, and repeats the legend of Washington's participation in the communion.

Colles names the plateau above Morristown Green "Fort Nonsense", telling us (if we read her carefully) that "tradition" says Washington himself gave it that name *"on leaving it"* (emphasis mine) because the soldiers had been employed there constructing a fort "to keep them from that idleness which was certain to breed discontent". It is possible, but perhaps not

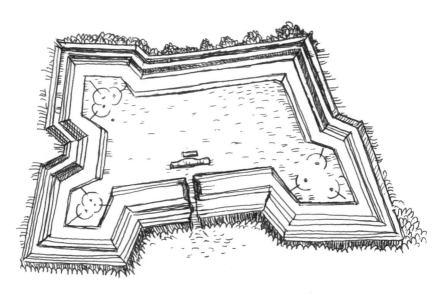

Fort Nonsense — the plateau above Morristown Green. Traditon says Washington himself gave it that name.

accurate, to infer from this that the fort was only "nonsense", or a waste of time in Washington's hindsight. The "tradition" that the fort was mere busy-work for bored soldiers has long been questioned. The fort is now thought to have been an important link in the chain of fire beacons, as well as a site for cannons to protect headquarters and, very possibly, the gunpowder stored near the Arnold Tavern on the Green.

Though Colles wasn't born in Morristown, she lived there at a time when enthusiasts of local lore found grist for their mills among the descendants of families who had lived in Morristown at the time of the Revolutionary War. She, and the other local historians of her day, did their best at the time to collect what they thought were facts.

This was true also, but possibly in a more studious way, with the next major contributor in the field, Andrew M. Sherman. His *Historic Morristown New Jersey* was published by a local printer in 1905. Sherman appears to have aimed at enlarging upon a booklet by Philip H. Hoffman titled "The Arnold Tavern" that appeared two years earlier. Sherman's lengthy and handsomely presented book includes some illustrations commissioned by Colles and used also by Hoffman. His is a discursive work, more like an avuncular fireside reminiscence than the factual study the subject required. Nonetheless, Sherman offers a valuable collection of local lore, some of it supported by documents then or subsequently available.

Like Hoffman before him, Sherman dwells at length on Morristown's gunpowder mill, which is not mentioned in the

Colles book. Sherman tells us that the mill on the Whippany River produced one ton of gunpowder a month in 1776,[23] and that the British General Leslie set out from Newark to destroy it in December of that year. This attempt was foiled by Col. Jacob Ford, Jr. (founder and part owner of the mill) and his battalion of militia who drove Leslie's marauders off at Springfield on December 14th.

Sherman writes that Washington chose the Arnold Tavern as his winter headquarters because of its reputation as a good and spacious public building. What Sherman means, I think, is that the Arnold Tavern was an ample public facility of some distinction, ready to accommodate the commander-in-chief and his staff immediately. A French visitor in 1780 remarked on the fine furniture and ample accommodations of the Arnold Tavern. In Revolutionary War times, that was an excellent recommendation.

Furthermore, the tavern was complete and wholly functioning, whereas the Ford house, whose exterior was so striking in a town with other large but plainer dwellings, had an unfinished second floor and kitchen facilities insufficient for Washington and a large staff.

Why didn't Washington stay in the Arnold Tavern in 1779-80? He may have preferred to be removed from the center of the village, as he was protected by an experienced lifeguard detachment. Or, perhaps this admirer of fine architecture felt more at home in the well-crafted, if incomplete, Ford house. It was Washington's practice to abide by the advice of officers sent ahead to inspect likely places for him to make headquarters. If he was dissatisfied with their choice, he informed them, as in his scathing letter to General Greene who selected as headquarters the unfinished, windswept Ford house in 1779.

Sherman, who knew the man's descendants, tells us Jacob Arnold was five feet, ten inches tall, thick-set, broad-shouldered, and a "staunch patriot".[24] He had owned the tavern barely two years when the army arrived. It was but one of his many enterprises at the moment. In the 18th century taverns were likely to be the home of the proprietor, his family and servants. On the main floor there would be a bar and dining room for the public, with possibly a space for what today we call "functions":

The Dickerson Tavern at the Spring Street crossroad below the Green, the place of Morristown's first settlement about 1710. It would have housed military personnel during the war, and it was here, after a trial in 1780, that Benedict Arnold was declared guilty of malfeasance – a verdict that confirmed him in his plans to desert to the Loyalists.

civic gatherings, lodge meetings, dances, trials and a post office. If the Arnold Tavern was such an ample place, why then, we may ask, was Benedict Arnold's court-martial in 1780 held at Dickerson's tavern on Spring Street rather than Arnold's? Almost certainly the answer is that in the 1779-80 encampment the Arnold Tavern was again completely occupied by military residents while the smaller, less public, Dickerson's had, at least, the public tap room available for the trial.

It would be enlightening to know who of Washington's military personnel stayed at the Arnold Tavern that second winter, 1779-80. It is strange that Sherman and others who appreciated the historic importance of the Arnold Tavern do not seem to have looked into its occupation by the military after Washington's 1777 winter there.

He does, however, describe the Arnold Tavern. It was 43 feet long and 25 feet deep, with a 20 by 25 foot rear wing. It had a wide center hall, with what even in Washington's time were called "parlors" on the south (left) side, and bar and gathering room on the other. There was a kitchen and an eating room on the first floor in the wing and, above, an assembly room. The wing was possibly added as recently as Arnold's purchase of the tavern several years earlier, and thus these rooms would have been new and attractive to public usage.

Tradition firmly states that Washington occupied for his personal use two rooms on the north side of the second floor: his

office facing the public square and his bedroom to the rear.[25] Twenty-six men were posted to guard the commander-in-chief and his headquarters. Unlike the 1779-80 encampment, when the "lifeguard" are identified by Colles as being posted on the hillock across the road from the Ford house or "in the meadow" (now Jacob Ford Village) beyond, we are not told where Washington's guards lived when he was at the Arnold Tavern. We do know, however, that they wore special uniforms and were otherwise distinguished from the other soldiers. Washington preferred them to be gentlemen, from Virginia, if possible. If in 1777 the lifeguards actually wore the white uniforms trimmed in broad blue designated for them by Washington they would have been a striking sight in and around Morristown Green.

Andrew Sherman records the "well grounded tradition" that Washington was seriously ill with "quinsy sore throat", an earlier, alternate name for acute suppurative tonsillitis, while at the Arnold Tavern. He writes that Martha Washington hurried north from Mount Vernon to be with him because of his illness. In fact, Martha Washington's practice was to join her husband in each of his prolonged encampments throughout the war, but it is true she did arrive that year at headquarters just as Washington's ailment was abating, and she stayed in Morristown after he departed in April. It is remarkable that Sherman is so accurate about Washington's illness early in March, 1777 because at the time it was, for obvious reasons, kept secret.

Washington encouraged his officers to gather their families with them, and so when Martha Washington and some of her friends were in the village there was what amounted to a "court", with parties and dinners at headquarters. He quotes Timothy Pickering's diary: "Went to Morristown, finished my business with the Paymaster, and drank tea at headquarters, George Washington and his lady being in the company."[26]

Sherman pulls together the threads of local legend and weaves them into a colorful tapestry of Morristown in the Revolutionary War, tempered by Victorian circumspection. (He is loath, for instance, to mention the names of the women he interviewed.) He records the hunger of the soldiers: "There was a time when all [the soldiers'] rations were but a single gill of wheat a day"[27]; and Washington peering in a hut and asking, "Men, can you bear it?"

Sherman mentions the mixed loyalties of the Kemble family, expressing the firm belief that they were all steadfast Loyalists. The Kembles came to Morristown from New Brunswick about fifteen years prior to the war and settled on a sizeable tract of land about four miles south of Morristown on "the Baskingridge Road". They made no secret of their Tory inclinations. How could they? One daughter was married to the British General Thomas Gage, and a son, Samuel, was the sometime Collector of the Port of New York and consequently a crony of Loyalist officials in the city.

Another son, the long-suffering Richard, tried to keep things calm at home and took Washington's proffered oath of allegiance although, says Sherman, "he, too, was without doubt a Tory at heart".[28] Another Kemble son, Stephen, was present at the British evacuation of Elizabethtown. Sherman records that the crusty father, Peter Kemble, was arraigned by Washington for

circulating General Howe's proclamations[29] but that Richard was able to explain away his father's transgressions.

Despite Sherman's negative verdict, there is no persuasive reason to believe that the Kembles in Morristown were malevolent Tories or, for that matter, unduly sympathetic with the enemy. Washington is said to have called on them. Their Anglican faith in a Calvinist village naturally would have set them apart and made them objects of suspicion. At least one Anglican-Tory from Morristown, Nicholas Hoffman, had been escorted to the enemy line. He was followed a few months later by his craftier wife, who had the foresight to stay behind long enough to gather her money, which she then took with her to New York.

The Kembles survived the war and remained in their home on the corner of present day Jockey Hollow Road and highway to which posterity has awarded their name: Mt. Kemble. (The "Thimble Mountain" mentioned by one modern writer is probably in fact Mt. Kemble.) It is interesting to note that members of the Kemble family subsequently forged cannon for the Union army in the Civil War.

These are the first published local records of Washington and his army in Morristown in 1777.

The More Recent Historians

We now broaden our study to include biographies and correspondence of the Revolutionary War published more recently. It is a rich ore; for these writings build on, and are also a corrective of, the pioneering research done in the 19th century. To introduce the Morristown encampment of 1777, we will begin with the events immediately prior to Washington's arrival in Morristown on January 6th.

Fresh from his defeats on Long Island, Manhattan, and Westchester, and with his army reduced to around 3,000 men, Washington needed to find shelter, food, and a strategic location in which to wait out the winter. Perhaps Newark, with its population of Puritan-descended "staunch Whigs who strongly supported independence" would be safe.[30] But the enemy skulked near Elizabethtown, and was well established on nearby Staten Island and New York City.

New Brunswick would be a better winter haven. It was farther away from New York City, but easily accessible by land and water. The army headed there, and Washington ordered the British-turned-American General Charles Lee to cover his crossing of the Raritan. Lee, however, had taken a leisurely twenty-three days to march southward in New Jersey after crossing the Hudson. He did manage to delay Cornwallis at the Raritan, but the British arrived in New Brunswick the next day.[31] Again, Washington was on the move, this time looking toward Philadelphia, though the Continental Congress had temporarily fled that city for Baltimore.

General Lee is said to have advised Washington to go to Morristown for the winter. Lee (not to be confused with the Virginians of that name) was an opinionated and loquacious officer, given to second-guessing the commander-in-chief, whom he had known in the French and Indian War. An English diplomat declared "Lee was the worst present that could be made to any army".[32] His best quality, and the one that must have appealed most to Washington, apart from Lee's experienced generalship, was his sincere commitment to human liberty. However, he seems to have felt this included the freedom to broadcast his low opinion of Washington's capacities as a general.

In mid-December Lee was in Morristown. (He may have stayed at the Arnold Tavern.) In any event, he took it upon himself to assess the suitability of the area as a winter camp. He had been ordered to move quickly to meet Washington, but Lee, always keeping to his own timetable, somehow found his way to Mrs. White's establishment in Basking Ridge and was kidnapped by a stray group of British soldiers who accidentally discovered him dallying there. Lee had just dictated a nasty letter to General Gates about Washington.[33] Interned in New York, he offered the enemy his military expertise, suggesting to General Lord Howe ways to defeat Washington. To his credit, Howe refused to speak to Lee.

Washington may have felt no great sense of loss in Lee's capture.[34] It is tempting to wonder if he wasn't less than emphatic about arranging for Lee's eventual exchange of prisoners, but the delay in Lee's release was more likely due to the fact that the Americans were in a weak negotiating position because they hadn't captured any enemy officers of Lee's rank. Furthermore, there was some question that the British might treat Lee as a traitor, inasmuch as he had been an officer in His Majesty's service. Lee's captivity in the city happened to be comfortable compared with that on the deadly prison ships and old sugar houses where ordinary prisoners of war were confined. Despite Lee's faulty record, Washington was finally able to arrange his exchange and gave him another command, for he needed experienced generals. However, Lee was cashiered after his miserable performance in the Battle of Monmouth in the summer of 1780.

Having at first brushed aside Lee's recommendation of Morristown and its hills as a safe winter refuge, Washington hurried his army toward Philadelphia. The story of his sudden turn-around, his midnight crossing of the Delaware, and his

Morristown's geographical area as depicted on the 1777 map "Province of New Jersey", divided into East and West, commonly called The Jerseys.

surprise attacks on Trenton and Princeton is well known. The brilliance of these strokes has always amazed historians. Even Frederick the Great was impressed.

Washington himself tended to give credit to his fellow generals. But there is no question that his personal appeal to the soldiers to remain in service six more weeks after their enlistments expired was a major factor in his having an army with which to fight the battles of Trenton and Princeton. It is possible that Washington advanced $500 of his own money for this extended service, and his gesture was reinforced by funds furnished by patriots of the Philadelphia Association.[35] And he would have pushed on to attack Brunswick had not the British General Mahood's hard resistance outside Princeton dissuaded him.[36] Where, then, would he go?

To Morristown. Lee was right: Morristown's central but secluded location was ideal. From there Washington could keep an eye on the vital Hudson River Valley forts, and on the enemy in Manhattan and Staten Island. There were other advantages, as well. A recent authority, Richard M. Ketcham, has written,

> *Morristown's geographic location was almost ideal. Only thirty miles from the enemy in New York and Staten Island, the village was protected on the east by the range of parallel ridges known as the Watchung Mountains, which stretched from the Raritan River to the northern boundary of New Jersey; behind them, Washington's lines of communication with New England and Philadelphia were secure, and he could watch for British movements out of New York and*

move quickly to almost any threatened point without interference... Here he would wait and watch and try to hold together what would remain of his army after the six-week bonus men [paid by the ad hoc *Philadelphia Association] left.* [37]

So, the army – exhausted and yet with well-earned high self-esteem – marched to Somerset and then Pluckemin and flowed on in several waves to Morristown. Thomas Rodney wrote in his diary that "Our army was now extremely fatigued…yet they are in good health and tough spirits." Washington arrived at dusk on January 6, 1777,[38] *not* the 7th as some historians have stated.[39] It was Washington's eighteenth wedding anniversary. Snow was on the ground.

At first, Washington didn't share fully this positive assessment of Morristown's safe location. He was eager to move. The day after he arrived at the Arnold Tavern he wrote John Hancock that the stop in Morristown was necessary only because the soldiers' "complaints and the great fatigue that they have undergone" made it necessary for him to go there. It was, he added, "the best calculated of any in this quarter"[40]; he would willingly move on, "though I confess I do not know how we shall procure covering for our men elsewhere".[41]

Perhaps Morristown's reputation as the hub of iron mining and assorted foundries was now superceded by something of more immediate importance: food. The prospect of well-stocked barns and pantries meant the 3,000 soldiers suddenly settled there could fare better. There was another positive: the deep vale called Loantica or, more appropriately, Spring Valley provided shelter for the officers and men who could not be crowded in houses. A second look at the map showed Washington the main post road that ran between the Hudson Highlands and Philadelphia. When he studied the map further, he would have noted another major route, the Old Mine Road that began at Kingston, New York, crossed a fertile farmland and, reaching the Delaware River, followed it southward. This would be a possible route of communication with Philadelphia, and would be useful for troop movement if the enemy should control the Jersey post road.

Washington did not intend to stay long in Morristown. But, for all his distrust of Lee, he soon agreed with Lee's suggestion that it would be best for the army "to lurk in the strategic hills around Morristown".[42] It has been stated that Washington had never before seen Morristown. This may be true, but he certainly knew the vicinity, if not the village, for Washington had been a guest at Lord Stirling's Basking Ridge mansion in 1770.[43] During the winter months of 1777 Washington decided to stay longer in Morristown, in recognition of a military tactic he had perhaps underestimated, though he must have seen it used in the French and Indian War: hit-and-run "skirmishes". Skirmish parties would fight off enemy soldiers sent to collect whatever forage they could wrest from the Jersey farmers. This would be a major characteristic of warfare that winter. The war might be won, after all, by harassing and exhausting the British. It was a vitally effective kind of warfare.

The words *forage* and *skirmish* are operative in comprehending the developments of that winter. Washington learned this as soon as he arrived in Morristown. Three days earlier Captain John Stryker's New Jersey Cavalry had captured wagons full of winter cloth.[44] The area west of Morristown, and on into Sussex County, helped supply the army with food, while the territory to the east was tempting to the British, because the army, civilians, and horses in New  York needed to be fed. When the enemy came into New Jersey to raid farms and confiscate provender, they were likely to be met with militia men. The ensuing skirmishes that winter led the commander-in-chief to reevaluate the importance of what he had previously considered the "unruly" militia. Boys who had shot rabbits from the bushes now used their skills to shoot redcoats from the bushes. It was effective warfare, especially since Washington did not have troops to match the enemy forces massed in New York, Staten Island, Newark and New Brunswick.

A new respect for the American forces was growing in British military circles, however; especially after its victories at Trenton and Princeton. Col. William Harcourt, based in New York, said of the American soldiers in writing to his father, Lord Harcourt: "Though it was once the fashion of this army to treat them in the most contemptible light, they are now become a formidable enemy". He wrote this at a time when Washington

was worried about the failure of the "Provinces" to send enough recruits for his "New Army". It is no wonder, then, that Washington did everything possible to exaggerate the size of his army. He soon began parading his soldiers on the Green and the drill ground lying just to its south toward what is now Maple Avenue. One historian asserts "he scattered his men in farmhouses for miles around Morristown and kept changing them … Even the shrewd country people who should have known better thought he had a large army".[45]

And his ploy worked – Cornwallis told General Germain that Washington had in Morristown an army of 7,000. He was certain that that great number of men couldn't "subsist long" in a village of Morristown's size.[46] Cornwallis might better have been concerned for British General Howe's situation in New York, however. At first it was thought the city was well victualed, but it was soon apparent that Howe was hard pressed to feed the much-increased civilian and equine population of the city. He had not stored enough food in New York, supposing an unresisting New Jersey would offer ample supplies through the winter if, indeed, the Americans hadn't given up the war before winter was out. His mistake became acute, as we shall see, after Washington announced his amnesty plan.

Where was Headquarters in 1777?

$\mathscr{T}$he first local historians had no doubts that Washington's headquarters in 1777 was at the Arnold Tavern in the center of town. Other historians are doubtful. One attributes Washington's residence there merely "to local tradition".[47] The biographer James T. Flexner declares flat-out, "No one knows what house was headquarters at Morristown during the winter of 1776-1777."[48] In this instance I think "local tradition" is sound. Arnold's hostelry would have been an ideal place for headquarters that winter. It was centrally located, and large, with a meeting room. We know it was well-furnished, and Washington liked, if possible, to stay in such places. If he had been quartered in either of the other two (much smaller) taverns in Morristown, or in a private house, his residence there would have been noted by the public after the war. Descendants of the owners would have come forward to claim their deserved fame.

The Fords, for instance, were proud Washington lived with them in their house during the second encampment in 1779-80, and as long as they owned it they were generous in showing it to visitors. In the early part of the 1777 encampment Caesar Rodney and his staff moved in with the Fords and lived with them in their large but unfinished home. Jacob Ford, father and son, died very soon after Washington came to Morristown in January, 1777. Rodney departed for his Delaware home immediately after, but the large Ford house, now owned by Theodosia Ford, would not have remained empty of American officers. Almost certainly, other military personnel took the place of Rodney and his staff at the Ford house, but it has never been claimed that it was Washington and his "family" in 1777.

Lacking any other claimant sites, and in the face of long and unanimous tradition, it appears that Washington's headquarters from January 6th to May 27th, 1777 was at Jacob Arnold's tavern facing the Green. As will be seen, I think it probable that Washington returned for a brief stay in July.

Having said that, it must be admitted there is no official document verifying that the tavern was headquarters in 1777. Washington usually paid rent and, upon departing, was likely to give a certificate of occupation to the owner.[49] However, he did not arbitrarily dislodge the owners. For instance, in 1779-80 we find him, his staff and servants residing with Mrs. Ford, her children and household help. Assuming that Arnold continued in his role of tavern-keeper in the winter of 1777 (for business was booming) he, his wife, Elizabeth Tuthill, and their three children may have lived in or near the kitchen, or in some ancillary dwelling on the Arnold property that spread back toward the present Cattano Avenue. Once settled in the tavern, Washington appointed his own kitchen and serving staff.

Washington reserved the bedrooms on the north side of the second floor. His aides were across the hall and, almost certainly on the third floor. Four to six aides slept in one room. One authority says there were eight or ten aides, all told.[50] Flexner imagines that:

> *Working quarters were cramped. Tables were gathered from around the building and borrowed from other houses to be placed so close together that the aides had to keep their elbows hugged to their sides. Everyone knew in general what everyone else was doing; laughter or indignation would spring up and fly across the room.*[51]

Washington selected his aides with appropriate care. Before appointing them he described the tasks expected:

> *"[T]hose about me [will be] confined from morning to evening, hearing and answering ... applications and letters".*[52]

Possibly a hundred or more letters and documents went every day by "express", north to the Highlands, south to Philadelphia, and to the various generals and lesser officers quartered in New Jersey towns including Pluckemin, Vealtown

(Bernardsville), Quibbletown, Westfield and elsewhere.[53] It was Washington's practice to outline "heads", or main points on incoming correspondence that arrived by "express". His aides would then draft a reply.[54] "The young men around him were encouraged to look over his shoulder".[55]

The aides in 1777 got on well together. John Fitzgerald was remembered as "an agreeable broad-shouldered Irishman"; George Johnston "exceedingly witty at everybody's expense"; Tench Tilghman "worthy and modest" – and very conscientious. "I cannot discuss business," he wrote to his father.[56] Tilghman was instructed to write to the Provinicial Congress every day. Robert Hanson Harrison, a lawyer from Maryland, had served as an aide since late summer, 1775.

Alexander Hamilton joined the corps of aides in March, 1777. Mrs. Theodorick Bland, a Virginia lady visiting headquarters with Martha Washington and others a few weeks later, pronounced Hamilton to be a "sensible, genteel, polite young fellow, a West Indian".[57] She also said the aides were "all polite, sociable gentlemen who make the day pass with a great deal of satisfaction to the visitors".[58] General Greene said that Hamilton's appearance at headquarters that winter was "a bright gleam of sunshine".[59]

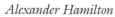

Alexander Hamilton

Hamilton merits special attention here if only because history has made him the most illustrious of the aides. He probably first saw Washington in New York as the General proceeded up Broadway on his way to Cambridge to take command of the army.[60] Hamilton was already enthusiastic about American liberty, but was noted for his cool demeanor among the patriotic hot-heads of Manhattan. Washington, for his part, would have heard of, and perhaps seen Hamilton in action in the skirmish at the Raritan.

He wrote to invite Hamilton to join his corps of aides at the Arnold Tavern on January 22, 1777 (Lord Stirling had earlier sounded Hamilton out to be *his* aide).[61] The appointment wasn't announced until March 1st, the day Hamilton began his duties. He was twenty-two years old. Washington's confidence in his ability was instantly demonstrated when he allowed Hamilton to draft a letter the first day. A few days later Washington became ill and Hamilton felt free to intercept a letter from General McDougall – he dissembled by claiming Washington couldn't deal with correspondence that day – and answered it himself.[62]

Washington credited his new aide with quick perception and accurate intuition. One biographer sees in Washington the father Hamilton thought he never had. Altogether, Washington had selected a good combination of men to serve as his aides. In time, the young nation would benefit from the lessons Hamilton learned that winter in Morristown. It says much for Hamilton that, though a newcomer among the aides, he soon became their leader without irritating the others who had served well and long.

The routine at headquarters was well established. Every day began with a General Order, and a new password. Important issues of the war were dealt with in daily correspondence. This orderly routine might be called truly seminal in solidifying and expanding Washington's position as commander-in-chief. We should bear in mind that his place in history was in 1777 far from secure. He had many military and political burdens. He was, in effect, in the employ of the Continental Congress and subject to "the dissensions and cowardice, the back-stabbing and avarice of the politicians in Philadelphia".[63] He also had to deal with a querulous New Jersey legislature and officers who frequently disappointed him.

Then, there were the administrative problems – food and clothing supply, policy and personality conflicts – which all needed to be deftly handled, ruffling as few feathers as possible. We are told about Washington's fierce temper, but it is his unending patience that startles anyone who studies his career. For instance, think how irritating it must have been to have John Adams, who was sensible but waspish, as head of the War Office. How maddening it must have been to have to publicly complain about having to pay and feed "vast armies" to maintain a thinly stretched ruse, while balancing on the brink of personnel shortages. What armies?

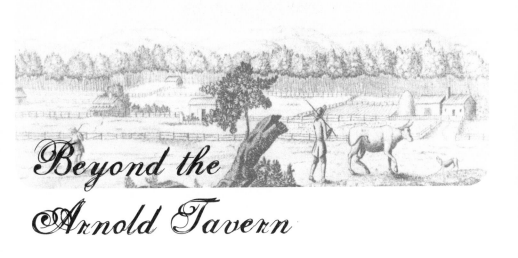

Beyond the Arnold Tavern

$\mathcal{O}$f course, there were officers and soldiers in Morristown that winter, and they did require feeding and clothing. The officers were quartered in available houses and, certainly, in Dickerson's and O'Hara's taverns. We are told that the forty or fifty houses that spread out from the village green were canvassed and asked to take in as many officers as possible. But if this is true, why is it that the descendants of those host families subsequently failed to pass down innumerable family legends?

There is a dearth of everyday information about Morristown during the Revolutionary War. Even privileged visitors who had been welcomed at headquarters provided posterity with a minimum of information for the record. We are left with little more than a few sparse mentions of parties and personalities at the Arnold Tavern. We search for stories from families whose lives were disrupted by officers intruded upon them, and find almost nothing. One historian says "the more accommodating" Morristown residents offered bed and board in their homes.[64] Maybe the householders in Morristown weren't as "accommodating" as the local chroniclers later on wanted to believe.[65]

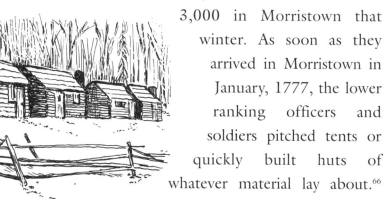

What about the common soldiers? Despite attrition there was always an armed force of about 3,000 in Morristown that winter. As soon as they arrived in Morristown in January, 1777, the lower ranking officers and soldiers pitched tents or quickly built huts of whatever material lay about.[66] Tent canvas was always a priority item for Quartermasters during the Revolutionary War.

It has always been believed that the main encampment in 1777 was in Loantaka, a mile or so south of Morristown Green. There is no

reason to doubt this. An old house still standing on the corner of Kitchell Road and South Street is said to have been a smallpox hospital. A man whose boyhood was spent in the next house claimed there were Revolutionary War uniforms in the attic. Whether we believe or disbelieve such assertions, they are founded on the long-held understanding that the army camped in Loantaka Valley.

It was a logical choice. It is well-watered and protected from the worst winds. Moreover, it is on the side of Morristown from which American troops could quickly turn out should the enemy from New York break through the Short Hills gap. Also, the site is partly protected by the Great Swamp. And the common soldiers were at a convenient distance from headquarters which, as we have seen, had its own blue-ribbon "life guard".

For Washington's army was hierarchical, as all armies tend to be. In the 18th century this took on a social stamp. Washington made it known that he wanted his officers to be "gentlemen". He meant men of recognizable family background, if possible. Those were the men who in his experience characterized leadership. His letters from headquarters state or imply the "gentlemen only" qualification again and again. He was successful in collecting presumably well-connected Virginians to be the headquarters' guards.[67]

Issues and Concerns of That Winter

Having, then, settled the army in Morristown, and seen something of life at headquarters in the Arnold Tavern, let us look at the series of crises in early 1777 that helped shape Washington's character as a military and political leader.

The dilemma of amnesty arose very early in the winter of 1777. The first notable episode was the commander-in-chief's independent response to one of Lord Howe's more intelligent efforts: his proclamation of amnesty on November 30, 1776. It provided that Whig citizens of New Jersey would be forgiven their former "disloyalty" if they swore allegiance to the Crown within sixty days. (November 30th is St. Andrew's Day, widely celebrated among the Scots to this day. Was this Howe's clever gesture to New Jersey Presbyterians? Quite possibly.)

The offer of amnesty was a wily move, as American fortunes were very low at that time. The Howe amnesty proclamation could have been a mortal wound to Washington, for he had been humiliated in New York and at the time was in retreat across New Jersey. Army enlistments would soon expire. Many militia men, practically independent of Continental command, had wandered homeward. Howe's proclamation must have been attractive to many people, and indeed it was in those days when the final defeat of the American "rabble" seemed imminent.

Howe trusted his offer would be approved by New Jersey residents who had opposed the Revolution. One of these, the Anglican faction, was centered on the deposed William Franklin, the Tory ex-governor. We have seen that Peter Kemble, an Anglican and an alleged Tory, was accused of circulating Howe's proclamation. Howe could also rely on the settlers of German and Dutch background in the Hackensack and Passaic Valleys. They did not favor independence. The Quakers were strong in South Jersey, and they also opposed war and tended to value the English as keepers of the peace. Morristown wasn't home grounds for any of these Loyalist groups, but there was always the probability that British spies were present. Further, there were Tories among the proprietors of the iron works in Boonton.

In his offer of amnesty, Howe had overlooked New Jersey's middle class: farmers, mechanics and shopkeepers whose Puritan backgrounds made them eager patriots.[68] Nevertheless, there were some people in New Jersey who, in light of the American defeat in New York, did swear allegiance to the Crown and received a document certifying they had done so.

Everything changed dramatically, however, after Washington's unexpected and wildly successful strikes at Trenton and Princeton. Few people knew of the close calls in both places, and no one could yet know the defeats in store for the Continentals, but some of those who had taken up Howe's amnesty began to have second thoughts. Nicholas Cresswell, an Englishman visiting in Virginia heard that the people in New Jersey were "all liberty mad again".[69]

Washington aimed to capitalize on the changed climate. He issued his own proclamation on January 25th, commanding and requiring every person who had taken Howe's amnesty to "Repair to Head-Quarters, or the quarters of the nearest general officer of the Continental Army or Militia … and there deliver up such protection, certificates and passports, and take the oath of allegiance to the United States of America". And then – note his exquisite tact mixed with burnished sarcasm – Washington proceeded to state that while he expected all citizens of New Jersey to be patriotic Americans at the same time he granted "full liberty to all such as prefer the interest and protection of Great Britain to the freedom and happiness of their country". However, in doing so they would be required to "withdraw themselves and their families within the enemy's lines", Those who did not comply within thirty days "will be deemed adherents of the King of Great Britain, and treated as common enemies of the American States".

In this instance, though, it seems that Washington wore an

iron glove on his velvet hand, for he was slow to exact penalties on unrepentant Tories. (Despite understandable occasional severity, Washington was inclined to mercy in the Revolutionary War. His compassion, however, was not as pronounced as was Lincoln's in the Civil War.) If a Tory head of household was notorious in promoting the Loyalist cause he might be escorted to the enemy lines. If his family chose to go with him they might take their household goods with them, and even be assisted in doing so by patriot soldiers (as long as the use of cartage didn't interfere with Continental army needs).

This unilateral proclamation by Washington was a masterful stroke. It officially reclaimed wavering families and rid some neighborhoods of troublemakers. The proclamation had yet another advantage: it sent Howe more civilians to feed in New York. These factors were overlooked at the time, though, and Washington's leniency infuriated many patriotic citizens of New Jersey.

Some members of the Continental Congress were quick to criticize the commander-in-chief. He had indeed in this instance acted unilaterally and thus lay himself open to criticism. For instance, on the day after he reached Morristown he was confronted by a vitriolic letter from the Executive Committee of Congress contrasting the bad treatment of American prisoners-of-war in New York harbor with the alleged princely treatment of British prisoners who were said to be "feasting on the fat of the land".[70] The blame for this inequality was laid squarely at Washington's door.

In a postscript to the letter, the States' delegates in

Congress questioned the form of Washington's edict, pointing out that an oath to a united States was "absurd" inasmuch as there was as yet no agreed confederation.[71] It should be noted here that Washington, early and habitually, wrote of the States as "united".

Washington stood by his amnesty proclamation. It was published in the newspapers datelined from "Morris-Town" (the usual style of writing). Perhaps he could afford to stand with his decision because, despite a dwindling army with few prospects of replacements in sight at the moment, the events of the winter had some bright aspects that enhanced Washington's authority. We will look at these presently, but first there was another major problem that snapped at Washington's heels that entire winter of 1777, the exchange of prisoners.

The question of prisoner exchange presented itself as soon as headquarters was established at the Arnold Tavern. It may have been complicated by the relatively comfortable house arrest (for such it seems to have been) in Manhattan of so significant a personage as General Charles Lee. Captured officers were usually paroled to private houses if they agreed not to resume hostilities until formally exchanged. The prevailing custom was to exchange prisoners-of-war according to rank: a private for a private, an officer of certain rank for an officer of similar rank. The Americans had taken no generals prisoner, so negotiations for the exchange of Lee were moot from the beginning. To further complicate the matter, there was a question of Howe possibly indicting Lee as a deserter. Nevertheless, Lee had friends

pressuring Washington to have him freed. Washington was given broad powers of prisoner exchange by Congress. He frequently corresponded with General Howe about the treatment and exchange of prisoners. In March, 1777 he initiated the first of several conferences with the British throughout the winter dealing with the matter, but there was little result. His courteous letters to Howe sometimes met a haughty response to "Mr. Washington" (for, to the British, he was an upstart traitorous subject of His Majesty, subject to hanging if captured). The British, furthermore, shied away from a formal exchange policy because it would imply an acknowledgement of American independence.

Washington's difficulties with exchange were exacerbated by complaints about the inhuman treatment of American prisoners held in the prison ships and former sugar houses at New York harbor. The prisoner's food ration was calculated as two-thirds that of an English soldier – and the English weren't known for feeding their armies well. It is thought that there were about 1,000 American prisoners in New York in the winter of 1777.[72] Lewis Pintard, a merchant in the city, was allowed by Howe to be an assessor of prisoner treatment there. It cannot be said that the British ever adopted a practice of inhuman treatment, but cruelty inevitably occurs during incarceration.

The bitter postwar memory of those ships and sugar houses was matched only by the reputation of the cruelty of the Hessian mercenaries in New Jersey:

> *"Wanton oppressive devastation of the country and destruction of property ... inhuman treatment of*

those who were so unfortunate as to become prisoners
... savage butchery of those who had submitted and
were incapable of resistance,"

described a Congressional committee on April 18th, 1777. The committee members doubtless had in mind what they had heard of conditions in the New York prisons, and what they as a fact knew of General Hugh Mercer's slaughter after he had been wounded at Princeton.

Another troubling question was the militia. This was a problem Washington had waiting for him when he arrived in Morristown in 1777. I have already suggested that in Morristown that winter of 1777 Washington learned to fight Europeans in a uniquely American way. We know now that the outcome of the war would be determined by endurance more than by dramatic head-on confrontation. How long could the British military and Parliament carry on a transatlantic war when threatened at the same time by strong enemies on the Continent?

When Washington and the army settled in their winter camp in Morristown, his thoughts were concentrated chiefly on what he called in his correspondence the New Army, for there was only a remnant of the "old" army. He sent commanding officers back to their States to recruit as many men as possible for three-year terms. He hoped to build an army he could depend upon; that is, an army centralized firmly under his command.

He had found the militia to be a fighting force he could not trust. The militia man's primary and emotional loyalty was to his

State; his commanders were likely to be friends and neighbors. Desertions were common in the militia – and understandable. These men had taken time off from farming to defend their homes. After a term of service, or even after a battle that seemed determinative, they thought it right to take time off from the army to return home to plant the crops in the spring or harvest them in the summer, just when wars were fought in the 18th century.

The commander-in-chief understood this, for he was himself a planter. When someone else complained about the militia's undependability, Washington defended it: "You must be fully sensible to the Hardship imposed upon Individuals, and how detrimental it must be to the Public, to have the Farmers and Tradesmen frequently called into the Field as Militia-men, whereby a total stop is put to Arts and Agriculture", he wrote less than a month after arriving in Morristown.[73] But then, the very next day, January 14th, 1777, Washington denounced to Governor Livingston, "the irregular and disjointed State of the Militia" of New Jersey, adding that it was imperative that the Legislature enact regulations "to reduce them to some order".[74] A particularly demoralizing episode was the Governor of Rhode Island's decision to enlist a militia whose responsibilities were limited to fighting in that State only.

Washington thought he saw sinister practices in the militia, too. Was it true that they "remain till they are properly equipped" and then run off home with their newly acquired firearms? Or proceed to threaten and plunder the civilian population, Whig as well as Tory?[75]

Still, despite his nagging resentment about a militia that acted as if it were beyond the control of the commander-in-chief, the correspondence from headquarters that winter shows Washington's developing appreciation of what the militia could do. Its nuisance value against the enemy was incalculable. At a moment's notice the militia could turn out and frustrate the British forage parties. This sharp, short, neighborhood fighting became the skirmishes for which that winter is remembered. At Springfield, Connecticut Farms and Woodbridge, for instance, the militia was effective in discouraging enemy advances toward the interior farm lands whose well-stocked barns Washington wanted reserved for his men.

If these were the soldiers who disappeared at planting time, they were also men who dropped the plane or plow and assembled quickly when the mid-winter call went out. One historian puts it bluntly: "The militia was effective at hunting, capturing and killing Loyalists".[76] Its nimble scrappiness that winter made Washington forget that the militia had practically evaporated in his retreat across New Jersey the preceding summer. The militia, in short, proved invaluable (and cheap) in running battles, harassing the enemy and essentially forming a blockade around the British army at New Brunswick. These facts, unfolding before Washington in the early months of 1777, eventually showed Washington the nature of the war he had to fight.

The operative word there is *eventually*, because in February 1777 Washington was convinced the British were about to move. He wrote to John Hancock on February 23rd, decrying "our delicate and truly critical situation for want of a sufficient force to oppose the Enemy, who are now ready and before many days elapse, will take the Field".[77] The same day he told Joseph Reed, "We are now in one of the most critical periods which America ever saw and because the Enemy are not in actual motion (by the by *I believe they are not far from it*) every body almost seems to be lulled into ease and Security".[78] And again on the same day, to General Schuyler, "I do not apprehend that the Petit Guerre will be continued long. I think Matters will be transacted upon a larger Scale". Incidentally, the facile use of the French language here may indicate Washington's full trust in his aide to compose much of his correspondence, for he had little or no French himself, but his aides Tench Tilghman and, later, Alexander Hamilton were fluent in the language.

Washington gave the increase of British forces near New Brunswick as his reason for anticipating action in the near future. Neither Washington nor anyone else could have predicted then that the British would be very late in resuming strategic action. He had to wait until late May, 1777, and that long pause in Morristown gave him time to adjust his mind to the kind of war he was waging, and to gather something of the army he wanted.

Still, Washington's alarm at a probable British move in midwinter is understandable because he knew, and was afraid the enemy also by now knew, the condition of his army. On March 1, 1777 he reminded John Hancock, "Our force is weak and trifling and composed of Militia ... whose service is on the eve of expiring".[79]

About the same time, Washington told Robert Morris that

the British had 10,000 men in New Jersey, and estimated his own force at 4,000. This almost certainly included "raw Militia, badly Officered, and ungovernable … It is with difficulty", he added, "that I can with every means in my power keep the life and Soul of the Army together".[80] He depended on the recruiting officers he had sent back to their States to bring in new men, but was often disappointed. In early March Washington wrote to William Duer (whose grandchildren would one day own the Kemble place), "The slow progress in the recruiting service gives me much concern",[81] and in desperation asked Governor Jonathan Trumbull in Connecticut to send militia men to help augment the Continental force stationed there. In the final analysis, despite frustrating experiences with the militia, Washington knew he needed those men, and he appreciated their efforts in keeping the British at bay in the winter of 1777.

Soon after setting up headquarters at the Arnold Tavern, Washington was faced with a problem that may seem amusing in retrospect, but that certainly didn't amuse him: French officers.

Silas Deane, the American emissary in Paris, was overly optimistic about awarding commissions and giving promises of command in the American army to French applicants who claimed soldiering experience. Deane was a habitual, cynical wheeler-dealer; in a candid moment he admitted, "I'm no more dishonest than the next man".[82] Such a man couldn't be gullible, so let us say he was perhaps hopeful about these gentlemen whom he met in Paris. In any case, as Henry Laurens said, Deane was unable to "say nay to any Frenchman who called himself

Count or Chevalier".[83] However, it must be said to his credit that Silas Deane promoted the aspirations of Kalb and Lafayette.

The result of Deane's caprice in Paris was the appearance in Philadelphia, and then in already-crowded Morristown, of "shoals of Frenchmen", as Washington said.[84] Congress and Washington were in a delicate situation here, because they wanted France to support the American cause. But that support didn't include importuning and possibly fraudulent Frenchmen claiming high positions in the American military. It was personally embarrassing for the commander-in-chief because he could not speak or understand French.

Here we have another aspect of the built-in problem Washington had with Congress: the constant threat of interference and the countermanding of decisions the commander had made, together with a lethargy or inability to be of help when it was urgently needed.[85] In the French officers *contretemps*, for instance, Washington complained directly to John Hancock that the French military "experts", tacitly encouraged by Congress, appeared at his office, exaggerated their experience, and couldn't possibly give orders to American recruits who understood French no better than did Washington himself.[86] Perhaps as a useful delaying tactic; Washington adopted the policy of requiring the French applicants to learn the English language before they were given command.

This predicament of French officers pales, however, beside what is surely the most devastating problem Washington faced in

Morristown in early 1777: smallpox. Smallpox was a scourge of the 18th century. It had the potential of killing an entire army, and the Continental army was already drastically diminished. The battles of New York, Trenton and Princeton, desertions and the expiration of enlistments had taken their toll. Now Washington had acute apprehensions about further losses caused by smallpox (Variloa), which was called the "King of Terrors" by John Adams in Philadelphia.[87] It was especially deadly among poorly nourished persons living close together, which description, of course, fit the Continental army in Morristown perfectly.

Washington had come down with smallpox himself in Barbados. He sensibly required his extended Mount Vernon family to undergo the tedious "Dimsdale method" of inoculation. This was the sole preventative measure he knew,[88] and the only one available until the discovery of vaccination years later. To preserve what remained of the army, and forestall the fears of new recruits, Washington made a quick and firm decision to inoculate. In a letter dated January 6th, he informed Dr. Shippen in Philadelphia, "I have ordered that the troops be inoculated". Since Washington is thought to have entered Morristown at dusk that very day, the letter is either misdated, or he and his aides worked into that first evening. Two weeks later, Dr. John Cochran in Morristown was directed to "use every possible means" to prevent smallpox from "spreading to the Army and among the Inhabitants".[89] As further precaution, new soldiers coming into camp were required to be inoculated prior to arriving. If the disease wasn't curtailed, Washington wrote, "Instead of having an Army here we shall have a Hospital".[90] He

spoke literally, for he knew the disease, and the aftermath of inoculation.

The process was tedious. First, the soldier was put on a light diet – nothing novel about that in this army. Then he was dosed with mercury, bled and purged. Then, serum from a pox vesicle taken from someone already afflicted was smeared into a fresh wound made in the soldier's body. The inoculated person was supposed to be kept in isolation. It is likely that it was during the isolation time that the camp "hospitals" and churches were used: the men were confined in those places after inoculation along with the others who had contracted the smallpox. The Baptist church, a stone's throw down the road from the Arnold Tavern, and the Presbyterian meeting house across the Green were used as hospitals and thus closed for worship through the winter and summer of 1777. In September, the Presbyterian congregation, having in mind its past winter of outdoor worship, appointed two Trustees "to wait upon some of the Docts. of the Hospital in Morristown & apply for an resignation of the meeting house and if obtained to apply to the Commanding Officer at this post to remove the troops thence & at [the Trustees'] discretion to proceed further in cleansing and refiting the House for Public Worship".[91] This action by the church Trustees indicates that soldiers in more or less significant numbers remained in Morristown throughout the war.

Morristown's Powder Mill

It has been said that the existence of a gunpowder mill was a factor in bringing Washington to Morristown in 1777. That claim may be discounted, but there was indeed such a mill. The existence of a mill in Morristown for manufacturing gunpowder was forgotten after the Revolutionary War except by the families immediately connected with the project. The little building fell into disuse, and in 1816 it was moved away from the Whippany River and made into a dwelling. Joseph F. Tuttle knew about the mill in 1850 and may have exaggerated its output and importance. Julia Keese Colles ignored the subject, but Philip Hoffman took it up and was given further information about the manufacture of gunpowder by a descendant of its builder. Andrew Sherman enlarged upon the lore, and provided embellishments supplied by tradition. It remained for Fred and Isabel Bartenstein to thoroughly study and give us an accurate history of the Morristown powder mill. Their findings were published in 1975.[92] Through the Bartensteins' efforts an accurate history and the exact location of the mill was made known.

During the winter of 1777 the mill on the Whippany River, about a mile east of the Arnold Tavern, was making gunpowder for the army. The mill is not mentioned in correspondence from headquarters, and its location, insofar as possible, was kept secret. A Loyalist newspaper in New York reported in July of 1776 that "a Powder works is now erecting in Morristown".[93] This notice would have arrested the attention of astute readers, for it was illegal to make gunpowder in the Colonies. The mystery of the source of the information remains – was it a Tory tip-off, or a Whig warning?

The Battle of Bunker (Breed's) Hill, June 17, 1775, had been a striking demonstration of the patriots' acute need for powder. Washington had informed the Continental Congress that the supplies of gunpowder were limited. Jacob Ford, Jr. – "very much a rising star in New Jersey's political and military sphere" – was a militia officer who recognized the scarcity of gunpowder. He was also an entrepreneur, and had experience in iron mining, which requires gunpowder in extracting ore.[94] Ford thus saw the military and economic possibilities of a gunpowder mill. He consulted with State and Continental authorities. The result was a loan of 2,000 pounds with the stipulation that the loan was to be repaid by powder delivered to the army. The mill was built in the spring of 1776 and was probably in operation by July. At that time Congress mentioned mills in Morristown, Rhinebeck, New York, and Hartford, Connecticut, producing powder.

A picture of the mill drawn a hundred years later shows a one-story building with an undershot wheel powered by water in a flume directed from the main river. Jacob Ford's land bordered the river but did not offer a suitable mill seat. Therefore, the mill was built on Daniel Lindsley's adjoining property. Lindsley was a patriot and member of New Jersey's

Gunpowder mill.

pre-war Committee of Correspondence that maintained communication about developments in the various Provinces leading to independence. He was not otherwise involved in the history of the mill, and died of smallpox in 1777. Lindsley's son, Joseph, inherited the land and became "the powdermaker".

Joseph Lindsley house.

But he could not have spent much time building or supervising the mill in its initial stages because he was in New York with "a company of Artificers" preparing the city's defenses against what turned out to be the very successful British invasion of the city by way of Long Island. From there he went on the expedition to Canada, departing the very day (June 21, 1776) Jacob Ford petitioned the Legislature for the loan. Subsequent service under General Lee and in Pennsylvania with General Sullivan meant that Joseph Lindsley wasn't in Morristown for any length of time until April, 1777, a month prior to the army's departure for the Bound Brook vicinity.

Jacob Ford, Jr. had died just after Washington's arrival in Morristown, so neither he nor Joseph Lindsley participated in making powder when the army was in Morristown. Ford's brother-in-law, and the co-guarantor of the loan from Congress, Jonas Phillips, became the mill's supervisor at the time. We can safely surmise that later Joseph Lindsley assumed management of the mill because it was on his land; he was deferred from further service in the army in order to work there.

Once the gunpowder was made it had to be stored in a safe place. The logical place in Morristown would have been near the headquarters of the Quartermaster, General Greene. We have always been told this was on the Green, equidistant between his quarters on its southeast corner and Washington at the Arnold Tavern. The center of the village was safe because it was busy with military men coming and going. Most of them would have recognized each other, and the reason for their presence there would have been known. Yes, it was known that spies were about, but a strange face would be noted. Andrew Sherman claims no enemy *other than* a spy or marauder ever came into Morris County in the war.

Once produced in the mill, tradition states the gunpowder was turned into barrels and carted to the storehouse by Benoni Hathaway. He lived near the Green. Later legend, which makes sense, said the carts were brought with a certain ostentation to town in order to impress any spies skulking nearby. And, we might add, to bolster the morale of the soldiers. A persistent story holds that when the supply from the mill ran low the barrels were filled with sand.

It may be questionable whether all the gunpowder was stored in only one repository in the center of the village. An explosion there would destroy the entire supply. Perhaps there wasn't enough gunpowder to require more than several storage houses. On the other hand, there is the post-war entry in the Minutes of the Trustees of the Presbyterian Church recording the church's purchase of "the Continental Buildings on the Parsonage Land ... for the sum of twenty-three Pounds."[95] The Parsonage Lands were on the east, not the south, side of the Green. Furthermore, the "Continental Store House" often identified as the O'Hara Tavern, was of a size that would have commanded a sale price of much more than twenty-three Pounds. The Minutes state that Quartermasters Obale and Ferman, presumably guards of the place, were still in residence there. This is proof that there was a military presence in Morristown as long as the war lasted. Probably, several buildings, a distance from each other on or near the Green, were used to store whatever gunpowder was made in the mill.

A further observation about the powder mill: it was planned and built in quick time in 1776 because, as we are told, the "American supply of powder was paralyzingly short in early 1776. The Canadian expedition was also shy of gun powder".[96] But by the time of the battles of Long Island and New York in the summer, "sufficient powder was available".[97] Since the Morristown mill was operating in 1777, Joseph Lindsley's deferment, together with that for several other men, from further service in the army, indicates gunpowder was made in the mill for some time, if not throughout the war. (Charles Hoff of the Hibernia Iron Works, which claimed to have made 120 tons of shot during the war was granted a similar exemption.)[98]

Washington surely would have inspected the premises when he was in Morristown if the mill in Morristown was a vital supply. The absence of any reference to such a visit, or any mention of the mill in his correspondence, leads us to conclude it wasn't very important. Furthermore, there is one historian's assertion that the army "never ran short of powder, flints and ammunition in the winter of 1776-77".[99] Robert Morris in Philadelphia, ever the optimist, informed Silas Deane in June, 1776, "We are better supplied ... our mills make it fast."[100] Did the Morristown, Rhinebeck and Hartford mills make all that gunpowder? No. The supply came mainly from France, at first by way of the West Indies. The plucky American privateers took it aboard there and brought it to safe ports. Before long, France would be bringing powder and arms directly to the States. Most of the gunpowder used in the American Revolution came by water.

The Local Scene

Finally, let us look at war's impact on Morristown. The best way to picture the local situation Morristown residents experienced in 1777 is to imagine a community of 250 people suddenly overcome by 3,500 military men. Ordinary civic life would be inundated. Homes would be disrupted by strangers who had to be fed and quartered. Barns would be requisitioned and some livestock would be driven off, while others would simply disappear throughout the winter. There would be slovenliness, and residents would be threatened by an overwhelming number of soldiers. "Washington's tired men must have found Morristown charming and cozy looking," one historian opines.[101] Perhaps they did, but they soon changed the village.

They appeared in great numbers, suddenly, in those first

days of 1777. They came by way of present day Green Village, or through Bernardsville. The march from central Jersey wouldn't have been arduous if the troops had enough clothing and footwear. They had neither, and this would cause the commander-in-chief anxiety throughout the winter. Often, the drying lines of Morristown dwellings would satisfy surreptitious military thieves who helped themselves to whatever they saw hanging there. (When Tempe Wick later hid her horse from larcenous mutineers, she was following the practice of experienced citizens who had learned their possessions needed protection.)

The Wick house

We have seen that the officers were billeted in homes and other buildings. "The houses in Morristown were warm enough even for Southerners", declares a historian from Virginia.[102] The common soldiers would not have been so comfortable in their tents, or even later when huts were built. Following the British practice in communities closer to New York, officers immediately canvassed the Morristown environs, listing from each household and farm what would be available to the troops.[103] This included cattle, grain and forage. Going from house to house gave a further advantage: it could detect the political loyalties of the inhabitants. Sometimes the interrogations became nasty, and then a farmers' food, cattle and wagons might be confiscated. At times payment was made, but often raiders hardly bothered with reasons or promises of compensation.[104] The majority of Morristown people were dedicated to the Whig cause and to endorse that majority, as Lt. James McMichael said, "Morristown girls are very fond of the soldiers".[105]

McMichael's comment about Morristown girls aside, there is little record of residents mingling with the military when the army was in Morristown. One family has a tray from which Washington, they say, was served lunch. The story is surely apocryphal, though it may point to hospitality offered. There is probably more truth in one family's legend that "the women of the family" constantly baked bread for the soldiers. Bread was made in every house almost every day; and there were soldiers in the house to eat it.

People must have seen the commander-in-chief, for he would take time off to ride out. Both he and Martha were skilled equestrians, and though he brought his coach to Morristown it is said he never used it. Still, there is remarkably little reminiscence about Washington in Morristown. Even the Ford family, with whom Washington lived for more than six months, had little to remember about the man's presence among them.

There is the tale of several Morristown women dressed in their best calling on Martha Washington at the Arnold Tavern. They said they were disappointed to find her plainly garbed and knitting, and inferred from her conversation that they should also be home, knitting for the soldiers. Today, the practice of searching for authentic "roots" is an accepted, even honored, pastime. It seems to have been non-existent in Morristown after the Revolutionary War. It was some time before wartime heroics and often dubious reminiscences emerged.

Washington's reserved persona is legendary. As commander, he "never pretended to be 'one of the men' and was careful to keep a distance between himself and his subordinates".[106] It is no surprise, then, that Washington stayed aloof from the people of Morristown who were characterized by one of his Virginia visitors as being "earnestest rustics".[107] This, incidentally, was the opinion of a friend who accompanied Martha Washington to Morristown and her letter, as one historian ruefully notes, "is one of the most interesting of the all-too-few gossipy communications from Morristown during the time Washington had his headquarters there".[108]

In the words of a modern authority on 18th-century manners, Washington "took for granted the differences between himself and the 'common run' of ordinary men ... He lived in an age when distinctions of rank and talent were not only accepted, but celebrated".[109] This observation helps us understand why frequent festivities in the Arnold Tavern that winter held by Washington, his staff and their guests didn't upset the soldiers whose lives in huts were far from celebratory.

Washington did well by his "family" of visitors and aides who worked and partied at headquarters. He appears to have advanced, and later claimed from Congress as a legitimate expense, about $1,000 a month for "Household Expenses". This did not always include payment to servants, one of whom was his aging, difficult, but apparently indispensable, housekeeper, Mrs. Thompson. He dismissed her because he considered her incapable of the domestic responsibilities at headquarters but, lacking a suitable replacement, he lured her back from

Philadelphia to preside again in the kitchen of the Arnold Tavern. It was no easy task. Washington kept a sumptuous table. One bill of $260 in March, 1777 was for five geese, nine turkeys, 30 eggs, a gallon of rum, two quarters of veal, a bushel of apples, a quarter of mutton, six trout, four pounds of butter, and "10 Gallons rum to put to cherries". There is also a charge for Jenny, a servant, and a shirt for Lanny, probably a serving boy. Washington also had with him his valet, Billy Lee, a slave from Mount Vernon.[110]

Meanwhile, the other officers and soldiers in Morristown probably grumbled about their privations. And, we may suppose, so did the people of Morristown complain about the inconveniences caused by a great number of uninvited guests among them. Time swept away their bitterness. One descendant much later went so far as to exult that her forefathers "had the privilege and ability to make admirable sacrifice on the altar of liberty".[111] That was a noble sentiment a hundred years after the fact, but not all Morristown people were so glad to have their pantries ransacked, their clotheslines stripped, their bee skeps stolen and their livestock led away. Perhaps the most enduring loss was when orchards were hewn down for firewood to cook and heat the soldiers' huts. It took an untold amount of cordwood to do this throughout the winter.

On the whole, however, New Jersey had been pleased with the Declaration of Independence. Nevertheless, Washington was warned (and would have been aware) that spies were constantly present. He was also told that the enemy planned to capture him, a rumor that had a sound foundation in fact. It was constantly

said that possible kidnappers were seen lurking around the Green.[112] Remembering the kidnapping of General Lee in Basking Ridge, special precautions were taken, and his aides ran drills at the Arnold Tavern for the possibility that kidnappers might appear.[113]

A wise military man must participate in duplicitous measures and, as one commentator has said, "Morristown [was] the cloak-and-dagger center of America" in the winter of 1777. Washington was adept at deceiving the enemy. He encouraged the British in their belief that there were far more troops in Morristown than in fact were there. He arranged for ostentatious parades and daily exercises on the Green, scenes that would impress a spy.[114]

We also know that Washington had his own informers. Early in 1777 he paid more than $8,000 for "Secret Services".[115] This was probably parceled out by Washington's bursar at this time, adjutant general Joseph Reed, to trusted individuals. Reed was a native of Trenton and a graduate of the College of New Jersey at Princeton. His loyalty to the patriotic cause came gradually, for Reed was among those who were more in favor of reduced taxation by England than full independence. But he warned Lord Dartmouth, secretary of state for the colonies, that taxation would drive the Americans to fight for independence, and of course he was correct. Reed joined the Continental army and is said to have been Washington's "favorite aide and intimate friend".[116] Washington gave Reed the sensitive task of seeing that advances from his personal funds found their intended military and political objects, for it is said, Washington paid his spies $50 a month, and $500 in advance.[117] Probably taking advantage of an immediate situation, he slipped General Greene an unexplained $78 on April 19th for the "secret service".

This may have some connection with the story in which Alexander Hamilton later claimed prominence. Washington instructed an officer, possibly General Greene, to prepare false "returns", showing a force of 12,000 men in Morristown "and with his blessings and a few guineas these papers fell into the hands of a British spy".[118] Hamilton's account is that he encountered someone in Greene's headquarters he suspected of being a British spy. With the canniness of his Scots ancestry, Hamilton left on a table in plain sight a list exaggerating the number of American soldiers camped in Morristown at the time. Then he departed the room on a sudden pretense. When Hamilton returned, the stranger – and the list – had disappeared.[119]

For all this cleverness, it must be admitted that Washington's spy network failed to give him accurate information about the enemy's military intentions as spring, 1777 approached. Contemporary military common sense dictated the resumption of maneuver and battle. Washington was variously told the British would march through New Jersey to Philadelphia. Or sail there. Or strike up the Hudson. Perhaps Washington recruited too many informers who were themselves either misinformed, or double-dealers. In any event he was not given accurate, definite information, and lingered with the army in Morristown. The commander-in-chief's impatience at delay is often suggested in his correspondence from the Arnold Tavern that spring.

The time came, in May, when the men, like their commander-in-chief, were eager to get on with the war or, we surmise, to return to their homes. The most reliable information advised Washington that confrontation should begin in central Jersey, and so he left Morristown on May 27th.

There may have been as many as 9,000 men in the army at that time, and spirits were high.[120] One of the last letters Washington wrote from Morristown that spring was to Col. Jeremiah Olney, who was to remain in Morristown. Washington ordered that:

> *the Guard House in the upper Redoubt should be immediately finished, and if you are not able to mount a guard in it at present, you should nevertheless make it the quarters of a trusty Sergeant and select party of men, otherwise if the Enemy, or their Tory Assistants, should have any designs upon the Town, or the Public Stores in it, their first attempt will be to seize the height and turn our own Works [against us]*[121]

Washington recognized the strategic value of Morristown, so near and yet so far removed from the enemy, and he wanted "Fort Nonsense" completed and manned by a permanent guard. Otherwise, Morristown was to be "lightly held".

If Washington supposed that he would not be returning he was mistaken. For Morristown would have a second opportunity, in the winter of 1779–80, to certify its claim to be the "Military Capital of the American Revolution".

Endnotes

1 "I feel mad, vexed", Henry Steele Commanger and Richard B. Morris, ed. *The Spirit of Seventy-Six*, Harper and Row, 1958; p. 485

2 "a vacant and nearly square lot", Andrew M. Sherman. *Historic Morristown, N.J.*, Howard Publishing Co., 1905; p. 67

3 "No grass grew on its face", Andrew M. Sherman. *Historic Morristown, N.J.*, Howard Publishing Co., 1905; p. 69

4 "a rude log structure", ibid., p. 68

5 "vegetables and some fruits", W. B. Allen, ed., *George Washington, A Collection*, Indianapolis, 1988

6 "supervised the jail", ibid.

7 "250 inhabitants, it is said", W. W. Munsell, *The History of Morris County, N.J.*, New York, 1882; p. 113

8 "anything to the army on credit", Bruce Chadwick, *George Washington's War, Servicebooks*, 2004' p. 130. Also W. B. Allen, op. cit., p. 156

9 "authorized by Congress", Bruce Chadwick, op. cit., pp. 129ff

10 "the Spanish dollar", ibid., p. 130

11 "earlier, in 1773", W. B. Allen, op. cit., p. 172

12 "though considerably altered", Munsell, op. cit., p. 115

13 "the trap door of their arsenal", Julia Keese Colles, *Authors and Writers Associated with Morristown, N.J.*, Vogt Brothers, Morristown, N.J., 1893; pp. 10-11

14 "materials placed in his hand", Munsell, op. cit., p. 108

15 "iron works large and small", ibid., p. 44

16 "wheels and other ironware", Chadwick, op. cit., p. 173

17 "side of the public square", Munsell, op. cit., p. 57

18 "headquarters in Morristown in 1777", ibid., p. 144

19 "by convalescing soldiers", ibid., p. 117

20 "Greene to succeed him", ibid., p. 118

21 "his neighbor, G. P. Macculloch", ibid., p. 119

22 "covering for our men elsewhere", ibid., p. 116

23 "gunpowder a month in 1776", Sherman, op. cit., p. 202

24 "a staunch patriot", ibid., p. 207

25 "bedroom to the rear:", ibid., p. 208

26 "being in the company", ibid., p. 221

27 "a single gill of wheat a day", ibid., p. 219

28 "a Tory at heart", ibid., p. 229

29 "General Howe's proclamation", ibid., p. 230

30 "supported independence", David Hackett Fischer, *Washington's Crossing*, Oxford University Press, 2004; p. 128

31 "the town the next day", ibid., p. 130

32 "this overstates the facts", ibid., p. 150

33 "General Gates about Washington", Richard M. Ketcham, *The Winter's Soldiers*, Doubleday and Co., 1973; p. 257

34 "in Lee's capture", Fischer, op. cit., p. 150

35 "funds furnished by patriots", Marvin Kitman, ed., *George Washington's Expense Account*, Simon and Schuster, 1970; p. 215

36 "outside Princeton dissuaded him", Fischer, op. cit., p. 340

37 "ad hoc Philadelphia Association", Ketcham, op. cit., p. 379

38 "at dusk on January 6, 1777", *George Washington in the American Revolution*, Little, Brown and Co., 1967; p. 342

39 Both Hoffman and Colles give January 7, 1777 as the day of Washington's first arrival in Morristown

40 "of any in this quarter", Dorothy Touhig, ed., *The Papers of George Washington*, University of Virginia Press, 1998; vol. VIII, p. 9

41 "for our men elsewhere", ibid.

42 "lurk in the strategic hills around Morristown", Flexner, op. cit. p. 293

43 "Basking Ridge mansion in 1770", John E. Ferling, *The First of Men – A Life of George Washington*, University of Tennesee Press, 1988; p. 191

44 "wagons full of cloth", Ketcham, op. cit., p. 280

45 "thought he had a large army", Kitman, op. cit., p. 219

46 "in a village Morristown's size", ibid., p. 380

47 "to local tradition", ibid., p. 6

48 "during the winter of 1776-1777", James Thomas Flexner, *The Young Hamilton*, Little, Brown and Co., 1975; p. 148. But why does Flexner suppose Washington had a house in Morristown in 1776?

49 "occupation to the owner", *James T. Flexner to J.E.L.*, January 22, 1971

50 "ten aides, all told", John E. Ferling, op. cit., p. 194

51 "fly across the room", James T. Flexner, *The Young Hamilton*; p. 147

52 "applications and letters", Richard Brookhiser, *Alexander Hamilton*, The Free Press, 1999; p. 29

53 "Westfield and elsewhere", Ron Chernow, *Alexander Hamilton*, The Penguin Press, 2004

54 "draft a reply", James T. Flexner, *The Young Hamilton*; p. 145

55 "over his shoulder", ibid.

56 "cannot discuss business", W. B. Allen, op. cit., p. 78

57 "a West Indian", ibid.

58 "satisfaction to the visitors", James T. Flexner, *The Young Hamilton*, p. 148

59 "gleam of sunshine", ibid.

60 "command of the army", Ron Chernow, op. cit., p. 66

61 "to be his aide", Richard Brookhiser, op. cit., p. 73

62 "answered it himself", James T, Flexner, *The Young Hamilton*, p. 139

63 "politicians in Philadelphia", Ron Chernow, op. cit., p. 90

64 "in their homes", John E. Ferling, op. cit., p. 194

65 In this connection I will state that though three of my family's houses adjoined the Ford property, and another ancestor was proprietor of Dickerson's Tavern, the only "lore" accumulated is the few incidents related to, and by, Hoffman and Sherman

66 "material lay about", John E. Ferling, op. cit., p. 195

67 "the headquarters guards", *cf. G.W. to Col. Caleb Gibbs*, April 22, 1777

68 "eager patriots", David Hackett Fischer, op. cit., p. 161

69 "all liberty mad again", Richard M. Ketcham, op. cit., p. 384

70 "on the fat of the land", Dorothy Touhig, ed., op. cit., p. 7

71 "no agreed confederation", James T. Flexner, *George Washington in the American Revolution*; p. 192

72 "the winter of 1777", Richard L. Blanco, ed., *The American Revolution 1775-1783*, Garland Publishing Co., 1993; vol. II, p. 1331

73 "arriving in Morristown", Dorothy Touhig, ed., op. cit., p. 131

74 "to some order", ibid., p. 147

75 "Whig as well as Tory", ibid., p. 121

76 "and killing Loyalists", Richard L. Blanco, ed., op. cit., vol. II, p. 1072

77 "will take the Field", Dorothy Touhig, ed., op. cit. p. 144

78 "ease and security", ibid., p. 433

79 "eve of expiring", ibid., p. 473

80   "the Army together", ibid., p. 488

81   "gives me much concern", ibid., p. 519

82   "than the next man", Richard L. Blanco, ed., op. cit., vol. I, p. 439

83   "Count or Chavalier", ibid., p. 440

84   "as Washington said", Dorothy Touhig, ed., op. cit., p. 378.

85   "needed that help", vide John C. Fitzpatrick, ed., *The Writings of George Washington*, and Dorothy Touhig, ed., op. cit. for numerous examples

86   "did Washington himself", *George Washington to John Hancock*, February 11, 1777

87   "the King of Terrors", David McCullough, *John Adams*, Simon and Schuster, 2001; p. 141

88   "measure he knew", Richard L. Blanco, ed., op. cit., vol. II, p. 1040

89   "among the Inhabitants", *G. W. to John Cochran*, January 20, 1777

90   "shall have a Hospital", *G. W. Letter*, January 28, 1777

91   "house for public worship", *Registers, Minutes and History of the First Presbyterian Church in Morristown, N.J.*, n.d.; p. 11

92   "published in 1975", Fred and Isobel Bartenstein, *New Jersey's Revolutionary Powder Mill, Morristown, N.J.*, 1975

93   "is now erecting in Morristown", *New York Gazette and Weekly Mercury*, July 7, 1776

94   "in extracting ore", Bruce Chadwick, op. cit., p. 176

95   "sum of twenty-three pounds", *Registers, Minutes and History of the First Presbyterian Church in Morristown, N.J.*, May 25, 1782

96   "shy of gunpowder", Douglas Southall Freeman

97   "powder was available", ibid.

98   "a similar exemption", W. W. Munsell, op. cit., p. 51

99   "winter of 1777", David Hackett Fischer, op. cit., p. 155

100   "make it fast", Richard L. Blanco, ed. op. cit., vol. I, p. 710

1777

101 "one historian opines", John E. Ferling, op. cit., p. 194

102 "a historian from Virginia", Douglas Southall Freeman, *George Washington*, Charles Scribner and Sons, 1951; vol. IV, p. 396

103 "to the troops", David Hackett Fischer, op. cit., p. 173

104 "promises of compensation", Richard L. Blanco, ed., op. cit., vol. II, p. 1217

105 "fond of soldiers", Bruce Chadwick, op. cit., p. 77

106 "and his subordinates", Stephen E. Ambrose, *Personal Reflections of An Historian*, Simon and Schuster, 2002; p. 10

107 "ernestest rustics", James T. Flexner, *The Young Hamilton*, p. 148

108 "his headquarters there", Douglas Southall Freeman, op. cit., p. 413

109 "accepted, but celebrated", Wendell Garrett, *The Magazine Antiques*, January, 2006; p. 143

110 "from Mount Vernon", Bruce Chadwick, op. cit., p. 78

111 "the altar of liberty", Andrew M. Sherman, op. cit., p. 384

112 "around the Green", ibid., p. 81

113 "kidnappers appear", W. B. Allen, op. cit., p. 81

114 "impress a spy", Bruce Chadwick, op. cit., p. 78

115 "for Secret Services", Marvin Kitman, op. cit., p. 210

116 "an intimate friend", *Dictionary of American Biography*, Charles Scribner's Sons, 1935; vol. VIII, p. 452

117 "$500 I advance", Bruce Chadwick, op. cit., p. 81

118 "hands of a British spy", Marvin Kitman, op. cit., p. 219

119 "supposed would happen", ibid.

120 "high spirits", Richard M. Ketcham, op. cit., p. 392

121 "our own Works", Dorothy Touhig, ed, op.cit., p. 549

Index

1777

Contributors to the Green Vision Campaign

Anonymous
Carl W. Badenhausen
Fred Bartenstein, Jr.
Sheldon Bennett Estate
Gretchen & Herbert Braunschweiger
Harry G. Carpenter
Mrs. Clifford C. Cavanaugh
Eleanor & Glenn K. Coutts, Sr.
Christine & Robert Cox
Donald Crabtree
Alice D. Cutler
Daily Record
William Dana, Jr.
Barbara N. Doggett
Barbara McClelland Day Dugan
Sally Epstein
F. M. Kirby Foundation
Kay & Frank J. Failla
First Church of Religious Science
First Morris Bank & Trust
Rodney P. Frelinghuysen
Clementina B. & Harrison Gardner
Geraldine R. Dodge Foundation
Kathleen & James G. Gilbert
James R. Gillen
Joseph P. Goryeb
Paula Gottesman
Sheridan & John Greeniaus
The Hampshire Companies
Linda & John P. Hellstrom
In Memory of Barbara Barrett Hoskins
Jo Anne & Joseph B. Howell
Helen & Henry M. Hoyt
Jockey Hollow Foundation
John Bickford Foundation

Dorothy Johnson Estate
Joint Free Public Library of
        Morristown & Morris Township
Allan P. Kirby, Jr.
Nicki & Paige L. L'Hommedieu
M. Blair & Gordon MacInnis
Albert W. Merck
County of Morris
Proceeds of Morristown Beautiful Campaign
Morristown Rotary Club
Town of Morristown
Joan & Morgan J. Murray
State of New Jersey
Baba & Franklin E. Parker
Peapack-Gladstone Bank
Jean L. & Aaron Rich
Cintra & Franklyn L. Rodgers
Nancy & Nelson Schaenen, Jr.
Schenck, Price, Smith & King LLC
Janice W. & Stuart D. Sendell
Richard C. Simon
The William E. Simon Family
Thomas Slutsker
In Memory of Shelly Smith
Clifford W. Starrett
Norman B. Tomlinson, Jr.
In Memory of Norman J. Tregenza
Mrs. George Washington, Jr.
Bonnie & Thomas P. Welsh
Kim & Finn Wentworth
Judith A. & Stephen B. Wiley
Kathryn & H. Michael Wilson
Wyeth Corporation
Dr. David O. Zenker